When Wood

Turns to

Stone:

The Story of the Arizona National Petrified Forest

By

K.S. Tankersley, Ph.D.

Little John Publishing, Inc.
Glendale, AZ

Little John Publishing, a Division of Southwest Training
Development, Inc.,
20118 N. 67th Avenue, Suite 300-159
Glendale, AZ 85308, U.S.A.

Paperback ISBN: 13-978-1500211080 and ISBN: 10-
150211087

Library of Congress Cataloging-in-Publication Data

Tankersley, K.S., When Wood Turns to Stone: The Story of the
Arizona National Petrified Forest/K.S. Tankersley
ISBN: 13-978-1500211080; ISBN 10: 1500211087

Table of Contents

Introduction

Did you know that dinosaurs once roamed the continent of North America and that the land in the American Southwest was once lush and green and not the grasslands and desert that it is today? Two hundred to 225 million years ago, during what scientists call the late Triassic era of history, the landscape in the continent that was later to become North America was vastly different than what it is

today. It was during this era that the changes that led to the creation of the Petrified Forest National Park began.

Millions of years ago, the environment in what is today the American Southwest was lush, tropical and green. The land was fertile and crisscrossed with rivers and streams. Tall, lush, conifer trees grew along the banks of the rivers and streams. Reptiles, like the crocodile-like phytosaurs and

rauisuchians, large amphibians, fish and herds of some of the earliest dinosaurs roamed the fertile lands in this part of north America. Although some were meat-eaters, many of these creatures fed on the ferns, cycads and other green plants plentiful in the region.

Although finding dinosaur bones in the National Petrified forest has been rare, the fossils that have been unearthed, tell scientists much about the late Triassic age. They know that the dinosaurs that lived here were mainly small

carnivores. The Triassic dinosaurs were human-sized and had long straight legs designed for bipedal running. They had small front legs that they could use for grasping their prey. Scientists believe that they may have traveled in packs to help them attack and bring down larger prey.

Scientists believe that these dinosaurs were plentiful here but not many of their bones have been found during archeological digs. The small and hollow bones of Triassic dinosaurs were like the bones of modern birds. The delicate bones of the Triassic dinosaurs broke down easily. Scientists believe they were not well preserved over time. The bones of dinosaurs that appeared later during the Jurassic and Cretaceous periods like the Tyrannosaurus rex or the large Sauropods, were heavier and more dense. Scientists find more of them because they are better preserved as fossils in North America. As a result, few dinosaur fossils have been found in the Arizona Petrified Forest.

Recently, archeologists have been targeting areas where dinosaur bones were more likely to have been preserved during their digs. This will help them learn more about the dinosaurs who

roamed the area during the Triassic era. Recent finds include phytosaur skulls and at least a dozen skeletons of the crocodile cousin, pseudosuchian archosaurs. Information about the creatures that lived here continues to grow as more fossils and information is unearthed. Scientists hope to learn more about this interesting period of time as they continue their work in the park.

History of the Arizona Petrified Forest

The Earth's Land Masses Shift

At the beginning of the Triassic era, the land masses of the world were still part of one giant continent known as Pangaea. The Triassic period marked the beginning of major changes that were to happen with the continents, the evolution of life

and the distribution of plants and animals. This
land mass had been located near the equator on the

NATIONAL PARK
FOREST

ALONG THE SOUTHWESTERN EDGE OF THIS REGION,
IN THE ARIZONA BADLANDS, YOU WILL FIND THE
WORLD'S LARGEST KNOWN COLLECTION OF
PETRIFIED WOOD IN PETRIFIED FOREST NATIONAL
PARK. MOST OF THE TREES IN THE PARK ACTUALLY
GREW IN DISTANT PLACES AND WERE WASHED TO
THIS BURIAL GROUND BY RIVERS AND STREAMS,
A PROCESS WHICH HAS TAKEN MILLIONS OF YEARS.
THE DECOMPOSITION OF THE TREES WAS SLOWED
BY A COVERING OF MUD, SAND AND VOLCANIC
ASH CUTTING OFF THEIR OXYGEN. THE ASH
SLOWLY COMBINED WITH OTHER MINERALS AND
SEEPED DOWN INTO THE WOOD. IT THEN
CRYSTALLIZED INTO QUARTZ, WHICH PROVIDES
THE WHITE AND GRAY COLORS OF THE FOREST.
IRON SUPPLIES THE REDS, YELLOWS, BROWNS,
BLUES AND GREENS; WHILE CARBON AND
MANGANESE FORM THE BLACK.
THE PETRIFIED FOREST NATIONAL PARK
OPENED IN 1962. IT COVERS ABOUT
100,000 ACRES AND IS LOCATED 30 MILES
SOUTHEAST OF JOSEPH CITY, AZ, ON US 180.

southwestern edge of the continent known as
Pangaea. The climate was humid and sub-tropical.

Pangaea began to break apart due to the sea floor
spreading at the mid-ocean ridge. As it broke,
it formed two large supercontinents. One was
named Gondwana. This land mass moved south

and contained what later became South America, Africa, India, Antarctica and Australia. The second supercontinent was Laurasia. It moved to the north and contained North America and Eurasia. While Pangaea was breaking apart, ocean and land plates shifted. Mountains formed along the west coast of North America as the continental plates were lifted by the ocean plates. At that time, the climate was very wet. Large conifers soaring 200 feet into the air grew by the river banks and the land was filled with lush, tropical vegetation.

The earth continued to change and shift its land masses during the Triassic Period. As massive tectonic plate shifts occurred, more land masses broke off and continued to push the new continents to the north. As it did so, changes in the environment and weather patterns took place. Volcanic eruptions covered the ground with ash and sediment rich in silica and other minerals.

The Forest Dies and Turns to Stone

The huge trees which had been up to 9 feet in diameter and 200 feet tall died and fell into the mud and ash sediment spewed by the volcanoes. The organisms and vegetation in the area died and were buried along with the trees. Over thousands of years, the climate transformed from the semi-tropical area that it once was to today's semi-arid grassland.

Rivers of water flowed through the land. The vegetation and huge, trees clogged the river channels as they fell. The river water became saturated with silica or silicon dioxide from the volcanic ash and covered the downed trees and plant life. The minerals in the water seeped into the cells of the trees and vegetation as it became buried in the silt, sediment and ash.

Buried under layers of sediment, the vegetation did not decay from exposure to oxygen and organisms as they normally do over time. Instead, the plant material was slowly replaced with silica, calcite, pyrite or opal from the minerals which surrounded it in the ground. Over millions of years, the cell structure changed and slowly turned into the stone fossils that we now find in the park.

People Arrive in the Land

Archeological evidence suggests that the earliest people to arrive in the Arizona Petrified Forest area came about 8,000 years ago. Spear points found in park excavations belong to the Paleo-Indian group. These people were believed to be a nomadic hunter-gatherer tribe. At first, they came to the area on a seasonal basis to hunt and gather vegetation. They camped in the area and hunted small game such as rabbits, deer, and antelope. They also harvested seeds and plants to replenish their food stocks.

In later years, these tribesmen planted corn in the area and built houses to stay year round. The early farmers first built pit houses on mesas or at the base of bluffs for safety. Later, they farmed the lowlands where there was better soil for growing crops. As climate conditions improved, they built above-ground houses, storerooms and multi-room pueblos in their communities.

A pueblo ruin of a 100-125 room pueblo dating back to 1300 A.D. can still be seen at Puerco Pueblo. At one time, this structure may have been home to as many as 200 people. The single-story sandstone block pueblo had no doors or windows and was built around a rectangular plaza. Entry into the village was by ladders over the exterior wall and across the mud roofs of the rooms. Petroglyphs etched into the desert sandstone mark the people's presence.

As the climate changed in the late 1300's, it became drier and colder in this part of the continent. Crops no longer grew well here. The people abandoned this location and moved to a more favorable location better suited for hunting and farming.

Explorers Find the Painted Desert

During the 16th-18th centuries, explorers looking for routes between the Spanish colonies passed through this area on their way to the Pacific coast. It is believed that they called this area *El Desierto Pintado* or the Painted Desert as it is still known

today. Spanish inscriptions from the late 1800's are found etched in the rocks on the grassy plains.

Exploration of the Southwest Territory

After the southwest territory became part of the U.S. Territory in the mid-1800's, the U.S. Army sent Army Lt. Amiel Whipple, here to search of an east-west route along the 35th Parallel. By this time, wind and erosion had uncovered many of the deposits of petrified wood on the valley floor. Whipple named the area Lithodendron Creek meaning *Stone Tree* Creek after the stone trees he saw here.

In 1857, E. F. Beale, a civilian contractor was hired by the U.S. Government to build an

east-west wagon trail along the 35th Parallel. Beale is best known for his experiment in desert travel that included camels. While camel travel across the country never caught on, the wagon road that he created was used by many travelers on their way west to search for gold.

The original wagon trail that Beale created can still be seen in many places across the southwest. Today it is on the National Register of Historic Places. In the late 1800's, settlers and private stage coach companies also followed this road on their way to California.

Since the area had rich grasslands, homesteaders and ranchers settled in the area to raise cattle, sheep and horses.

The Crossroads of East to West

The Atlantic and Pacific Railway was built to join east to west. The railroad led to the founding of towns like Holbrook and Adamana. Visitors could stay in Adamana and tour the Petrified Forest. During this time, the Petrified Forest was called the Chalcedony Forest.

When automobiles became popular, Beale's original route became the path of U.S. Route 66. This was a transcontinental highway developed in 1926 to help speed east-west automobile travel. This road was a popular and colorful route for travelers going across the country. Route 66 was decommissioned in 1985 to make way for Interstate 40 which still follows a similar path. The BNSF railway also follows this same route from the east to the west.

The Land Becomes a National Park

As travelers to the area increased, more and more of the petrified wood was disappearing. It was being taken for souvenirs and commercial use.

Local residents became alarmed by how fast the petrified wood was disappearing from the area. In 1895, the Arizona Territorial Legislature asked the U.S. Congress to preserve the area as a National

Park. Their first attempt to preserve the park failed. In 1906, President Theodore Roosevelt created the Petrified Forest National Monument preserving the park and its treasures for future generations. Making the area a National Monument made it illegal for people to take the petrified wood out of the park area so the unique formations would no longer be in danger of being lost.

Between 1934 and 1942, the federal workers of the Civilian Conservation Corps, or CCC, build roads, trails and buildings inside the monument area. The government also bought the land containing the Painted Desert section of the park to expand the land area.

The monument finally became a national park in 1962. The Wilderness Act signed by President Lyndon B. Johnson in 1964 set aside wilderness areas in the park to limit human activity to keep the land better preserved. In 2004, President G.W. Bush signed a bill doubling the park from 93,353 acres or 146 square miles (378 km^2) to 218,533 acres or 341 square miles (884 km^2). This is its current size.

Petrified Forest National Park Today

Today, the park is visited by more than 600,000 visitors per year. Some hike, many take pictures and examine the beautiful colors of the petrified wood. Still others enjoy learning about the history of the area in the Park Visitor's Centers. The park is located near the town of Holbrook in northeastern Arizona.

How Did the Trees Become Petrified?

The term *petrified* comes from the Greek word *petro* meaning *rock* or *stone*. This is the process of a tree or large plant becoming fossilized by turning into stone. While some fossils are just impressions

which have been left in the stone, petrified wood is an actual, 3-dimensional, replica of the original organic matter. When an object becomes petrified, it can preserve the original structure of the matter down to the microscopic level. For example, you can still see tree rings in a cross-section of a petrified tree log just as they were when the tree was still alive.

When the volcanos erupted in this area millions of years ago, the large trees in the dense forest that once grew here were destroyed by the hot ash and fire. They died and their trunks fell into the streams and rivers. They were quickly covered over by ash and sediment. Because they were stuck in the deep mud, no air could get to the trees original cells so they did not decay.

After the trees and vegetation die, the cellulose cells die. When the cells die, the inside of the cell becomes hollow. Water seeps into the tree and into the dead cell walls and fills up the cell. The minerals in the water fill up the cell.

Volcanic ash has a high amount of the minerals such as silicon, calcite, pyrite or other inorganic materials such as opal. As the water entering the cells evaporates, it leaves the minerals behind, filling up the cells. As the mineral dries, it hardens

into the stone-like substance that makes up a petrified tree. It still looks like the original, organic matter which used to be a tree but now it has become a solid and hard rock.

If you see a tree fossil that has turned all white or mostly white, this means that the water that filled the tree's original cells contained a high amount of calcium. Dark areas in the surface may have been caused by discoloration due to sunlight. In the Petrified Forest National Park, many of the trees have retained their natural colors. This is because the water that entered the tree cells contained a high amount of silicon instead of calcite. When the fossil contains higher concentrations of silicon, the tree remains darker in color.

Petrification is a natural process that can form fossils out of any plant or animal when it soaks over a long period of time in water that contains chemicals like opal, calcite (calcium carbonate), silicon or carnotite. Scientists observe that petrification happens more often to wood than it does to animals or non-woody plants.

What Colors Are in Petrified Wood?

In the National Petrified Forest in Arizona, much of the wood has retained its warm brown color due to the silicon in the water. Petrified wood may be a deep red, brown or orange if there was iron oxide in the water.

Carbon in the water might turn the petrified stone black. Cobalt, chromium or copper can give the petrified stone a green or blue tint. Manganese can turn the stone a pink or orange hue. Manganese oxides can give the fossil blackish yellow colors. When a fossil contains carnotite, we may see lemon-yellow areas in the petrified stone.

Petrified wood is four times as hard as granite and is very colorful due to its mineral content. Scientists observe that since the stone has high silica content, it is similar to agate in composition and appearance.

In addition to the petrified wood that is abundant in the park, visitors can also see the beautiful landscape in the Painted Desert. This colorful desert valley has a variety of hues and shadings depending upon the mineral content of the area. The layers of sediment and landforms in the Painted Desert were created by the Triassic River system as it flowed through this area millions of years ago.

Where Can Petrified Wood Be Found?

The Petrified National Forest Park is located in northern Arizona near the city of Holbrook, Arizona on the eastern side of the state. It covers about 230 square miles of land. While the Petrified National Forest has many unique characteristics such as the Painted Desert, it is by no means the only place to find petrified wood.

Petrified wood is not rare. Petrified wood can be found in the states of Louisiana, Texas, Mississippi, Washington State, California, New York, Wisconsin, Colorado, Oregon, Utah, South Dakota and near Yellowstone, Wyoming. It can also be found in other countries all around the world.

Preserving Our National Treasure

Taking pieces of the petrified wood as souvenirs or for use as furniture or jewelry is not new. Military survey parties passing through the region in the 1850's filled their saddlebags with as much petrified wood as they could carry. Petrified logs were carried off in huge quantities to be used

as tables, lamps and other pieces of furniture. To protect this special treasure, the area was declared a National Monument in 1906.

Despite stiff fines of $325 and up for removal or damage to the petrified wood or other natural cultural artifacts in the park, the National Park Service estimates that about a ton of petrified wood per month is stolen from the National Park.

Outside the park, there are many commercial vendors who sell petrified wood that has been gathered from private lands and not the National Park. This is a better way to take home souvenirs of your visit to this special national park.

Every year, a large quantity of wood is mailed
back to Park officials by people who have a guilty
conscience over stealing the petrified wood pieces.
Near the southern entrance, there is a large pile of
conscience rocks where returned or seized rocks

have been placed in a pile. The Rainbow Forest Museum has a large display of letters from people all over the world who have returned rocks that were stolen from the park.

Some people even believe that they have been cursed as a result of taking the rock from the National Park. They believe their bad luck began when they stole the rock from the park.

They hope returning it will reverse their bad luck. Although there is no evidence of any real curse being tied to stealing the rocks out of the Petrified Forest, it does do great harm to the work scientists are trying to do within the Park and prevents others from being able to see these special fossils.

Even though archaeologists are glad to see the stones returned, the harm done cannot be undone.

They say that once the piece has been removed from its original location, it can no longer be of any value in learning more about life during the Triassic period or even life during the Pueblo Indian times.

If you travel to the park, be sure to enjoy the beautiful sights and touch the pieces of petrified wood as much as you want. Since they are solid stone, touching their brilliant, beautiful colors will not hurt them. After doing that, please leave these valuable pieces of history exactly where they are so that future generations may continue to enjoy them and scientists can continue to learn about our earth's history and development.

About the Author

K.S. Tankersley has been a teacher and school administrator for over 30 years. She has worked tirelessly to help children succeed academically, learn about their world and be fit and healthy. She is a grand-mother of 5 and proud "mom" to two beautiful yorkies. She loves to read and travel whenever possible. She enjoys writing and sharing the knowledge she has gained on many topics over the years.

Other Books in the Exploring Nature Series by K.S. Tankersley

Amazingly Awesome Snails!
Sea Turtles: Amazing Giants of the Sea
Kangaroos Down Under
Discover the Koala
The American Black Bear

Available at your favorite book retailer in both paperback and ebook formats.

Made in the USA
Middletown, DE
10 October 2023

40588154R00027